WHAT DID I EAT TODAY?

A Food Lover's Journal

Kate Bingaman-Burt

Bake BON APPETIT Snack
FRY ROAST SAUTÉ

FORK

IF FOUND PLEASE RETURN

TO: _____

REWARD: _____

Yum
Yum
Yum
Yum
Yum
Yum

BAKE
BOIL

SUGAR SALT SIZZLE

KNIFE GRILL TEASPOON

PLATE SNACK

BRUNCH Steam

BRAISE BITE SUGAR PINT

HOW TO USE THIS JOURNAL

F ood is easy to talk about, write about, take photos of, complain about, and rave about. And, of course, food is also quite easy to eat. This journal is a celebration of both the *eating of* and the *talking about* food—in all its savory ups and downs and sweet ins and outs.

Fun things happen when you start to answer the simple question, "What did I eat today?" We might love to eat, but sometimes the true joys that we receive from food get lost in the daily grind. This journal is designed to help you rediscover those joys and think about the common threads that emerge in your daily chow-downs.

Approach the pages of this book as you would a dream journal; you don't *have* to fill it in every day, but the more you get in the habit of using it, the more useful and fun it will become. Simply log the date, the location, the food you ate, and any thoughts about the experience. You'll also find plenty of room to draw and doodle, and a variety of pages and prompts to help you expound upon all the glorious things that you will eat— today, tomorrow, next week, and onward.

TOASTED
BAGEL
w/SCHMEAR

WHAT I ATE: ....

WHEN + WHERE: ....

NOTES: ....

_____

WHAT I ATE: ....

WHEN + WHERE: ....

NOTES: ....

_____

WHAT I ATE: ....

WHEN + WHERE: ....

NOTES: ....

_____

WHAT I ATE: ....

WHEN + WHERE: ....

NOTES: ....

_____

WHAT I ATE: ....

WHEN + WHERE: ....

NOTES: ....

_____

WHAT I ATE: ....

WHEN + WHERE: ....

NOTES: ....

_____

WHAT I ATE: ....

WHEN + WHERE: ....

NOTES: ....

_____

WHAT I ATE: ....

WHEN + WHERE: ....

NOTES: ....

_____

avocado

WHAT I ATE: ....

WHEN + WHERE: ....

NOTES: ....

_____

WHAT I ATE: ....

WHEN + WHERE: ....

NOTES: ....

_____

WHAT I ATE: ....

WHEN + WHERE: ....

NOTES: ....

_____

WHAT I ATE: ....

WHEN + WHERE: ....

NOTES: ....

_____

WHAT I ATE: ....

WHEN + WHERE: ....

NOTES: ....

_____

WHAT I ATE: ....

WHEN + WHERE: ....

NOTES: ....

_____

WHAT I ATE: ....

WHEN + WHERE: ....

NOTES: ....

_____

WHAT I ATE: ....

WHEN + WHERE: ....

NOTES: ....

_____

LOCALS ONLY

*Food Challenge: Try to eat only
locally sourced foods for the entire day.*

BREAKFAST: ....

FROM: ....

LUNCH: ....

FROM: ....

DINNER: ....

FROM: ....

SNACKS: ....

FROM: ....

NOTES: ....

....

....

....

PUMPKIN
SPICE LATTE

WHAT I ATE: ....

WHEN + WHERE: ....

NOTES: ....

_____

, WHAT I ATE: ....

WHEN + WHERE: ....

NOTES: ....

_____

WHAT I ATE: ....

WHEN + WHERE: ....

NOTES: ....

_____

WHAT I ATE: ....

WHEN + WHERE: ....

NOTES: ....

_____

WHAT I ATE: ....

WHEN + WHERE: ....

NOTES: ....

_____

WHAT I ATE: ....

WHEN + WHERE: ....

NOTES: ....

_____

WHAT I ATE: ....

WHEN + WHERE: ....

NOTES: ....

_____

WHAT I ATE: ....

WHEN + WHERE: ....

NOTES: ....

_____

WHAT I ATE: ....

WHEN + WHERE: ....

NOTES: ....

_____

WHAT I ATE: ....

WHEN + WHERE: ....

NOTES: ....

_____

WHAT I ATE: ....

WHEN + WHERE: ....

NOTES: ....

_____

WHAT I ATE: ....

WHEN + WHERE: ....

NOTES: ....

_____

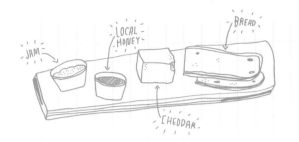

WHAT I ATE: ....

WHEN + WHERE: ....

NOTES: ....

_____

WHAT I ATE: ....

WHEN + WHERE: ....

NOTES: ....

_____

WHAT I ATE: ....

WHEN + WHERE: ....

NOTES: ....

_____

WHAT I ATE: ....

WHEN + WHERE: ....

NOTES: ....

_____

COCKTAIL HOUR

*Hunt down recipes for your favorite
cocktails and try them at home.*

COCKTAIL: ....

RECIPE: ....

....

....

COCKTAIL: ....

RECIPE: ....

....

....

NOTES: ....

....

....

....

WHAT I ATE: ....

WHEN + WHERE: ....

NOTES: ....

_____

WHAT I ATE: ....

WHEN + WHERE: ....

NOTES: ....

_____

WHAT I ATE: ....

WHEN + WHERE: ....

NOTES: ....

_____

WHAT I ATE: ....

WHEN + WHERE: ....

NOTES: ....

_____

WHAT I ATE: ....

WHEN + WHERE: ....

NOTES: ....

_____

WHAT I ATE: ....

WHEN + WHERE: ....

NOTES: ....

_____

WHAT I ATE: ....

WHEN + WHERE: ....

NOTES: ....

_____

WHAT I ATE: ....

WHEN + WHERE: ....

NOTES: ....

_____

WHAT I ATE: ....

WHEN + WHERE: ....

NOTES: ....

_____

WHAT I ATE: ....

WHEN + WHERE: ....

NOTES: ....

_____

WHAT I ATE: ....

WHEN + WHERE: ....

NOTES: ....

_____

WHAT I ATE: ....

WHEN + WHERE: ....

NOTES: ....

_____

WHAT I ATE: ....

WHEN + WHERE: ....

NOTES: ....

_____

WHAT I ATE: ....

WHEN + WHERE: ....

NOTES: ....

_____

WHAT I ATE: ....

WHEN + WHERE: ....

NOTES: ....

_____

WHAT I ATE: ....

WHEN + WHERE: ....

NOTES: ....

_____

ESSENTIALS

What favorite foods can you not live without?
Plan an entire day's meals around them.

BREAKFAST: ....

....

....

LUNCH: ....

....

....

DINNER: ....

....

SNACKS: ....

....

WHAT I ATE: ....

WHEN + WHERE: ....

NOTES: ....

_____

WHAT I ATE: ....

WHEN + WHERE: ....

NOTES: ....

_____

WHAT I ATE: ....

WHEN + WHERE: ....

NOTES: ....

_____

WHAT I ATE: ....

WHEN + WHERE: ....

NOTES: ....

_____

GRilled
CheEse

WHAT I ATE: ....

WHEN + WHERE: ....

NOTES: ....

_____

WHAT I ATE: ....

WHEN + WHERE: ....

NOTES: ....

_____

WHAT I ATE: ....

WHEN + WHERE: ....

NOTES: ....

_____

WHAT I ATE: ....

WHEN + WHERE: ....

NOTES: ....

_____

WHAT I ATE: ....

WHEN + WHERE: ....

NOTES: ....

_____

WHAT I ATE: ....

WHEN + WHERE: ....

NOTES: ....

_____

WHAT I ATE: ....

WHEN + WHERE: ....

NOTES: ....

_____

WHAT I ATE: ....

WHEN + WHERE: ....

NOTES: ....

_____

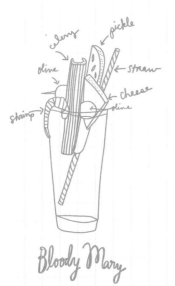

celery

pickle

olive

← straw

← cheese

shrimp →

olive

Bloody Mary

WHAT I ATE: ....

WHEN + WHERE: ....

NOTES: ....

_____

WHAT I ATE: ....

WHEN + WHERE: ....

NOTES: ....

_____

WHAT I ATE: ....

WHEN + WHERE: ....

NOTES: ....

_____

WHAT I ATE: ....

WHEN + WHERE: ....

NOTES: ....

_____

STILL LIFE

*Sharpen your pencils and draw the best
and worst meals you've ever eaten.*

THE BEST:

_____

THE WORST:

WHAT I ATE: ....

WHEN + WHERE: ....

NOTES: ....

_____

WHAT I ATE: ....

WHEN + WHERE: ....

NOTES: ....

_____

WHAT I ATE: ....

WHEN + WHERE: ....

NOTES: ....

_____

WHAT I ATE: ....

WHEN + WHERE: ....

NOTES: ....

_____

WHAT I ATE: ....

WHEN + WHERE: ....

NOTES: ....

_____

WHAT I ATE: ....

WHEN + WHERE: ....

NOTES: ....

_____

WHAT I ATE: ....

WHEN + WHERE: ....

NOTES: ....

_____

WHAT I ATE: ....

WHEN + WHERE: ....

NOTES: ....

_____

WHAT I ATE: ....

WHEN + WHERE: ....

NOTES: ....

_____

WHAT I ATE: ....

WHEN + WHERE: ....

NOTES: ....

_____

WHAT I ATE: ....

WHEN + WHERE: ....

NOTES: ....

_____

WHAT I ATE: ....

WHEN + WHERE: ....

NOTES: ....

_____

WHAT I ATE: ....

WHEN + WHERE: ....

NOTES: ....

_____

WHAT I ATE: ....

WHEN + WHERE: ....

NOTES: ....

_____

WHAT I ATE: ....

WHEN + WHERE: ....

NOTES: ....

_____

WHAT I ATE: ....

WHEN + WHERE: ....

NOTES: ....

_____

MAKE IT HAPPEN

Make a meal you've never tried before.

MEAL: ....

NEW INGREDIENTS BOUGHT: ....

....

....

INGREDIENTS ALREADY OWNED: ....

....

....

RECIPE: ....

....

....

....

....

WHAT I ATE: ....

WHEN + WHERE: ....

NOTES: ....

_____

WHAT I ATE: ....

WHEN + WHERE: ....

NOTES: ....

_____

WHAT I ATE: ....

WHEN + WHERE: ....

NOTES: ....

_____

WHAT I ATE: ....

WHEN + WHERE: ....

NOTES: ....

_____

APRICOTS
from the FARMERS' MARKET.

WHAT I ATE: ....

WHEN + WHERE: ....

NOTES: ....

_____

WHAT I ATE: ....

WHEN + WHERE: ....

NOTES: ....

_____

WHAT I ATE: ....

WHEN + WHERE: ....

NOTES: ....

_____

WHAT I ATE: ....

WHEN + WHERE: ....

NOTES: ....

_____

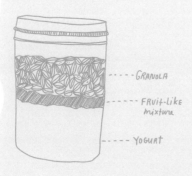

GRANOLA

FRUit-like
mixture

YOGURT

WHAT I ATE: ....

WHEN + WHERE: ....

NOTES: ....

_____

WHAT I ATE: ....

WHEN + WHERE: ....

NOTES: ....

_____

WHAT I ATE: ....

WHEN + WHERE: ....

NOTES: ....

_____

WHAT I ATE: ....

WHEN + WHERE: ....

NOTES: ....

_____

WHAT I ATE: ....

WHEN + WHERE: ....

NOTES: ....

_____

WHAT I ATE: ....

WHEN + WHERE: ....

NOTES: ....

_____

WHAT I ATE: ....

WHEN + WHERE: ....

NOTES: ....

_____

WHAT I ATE: ....

WHEN + WHERE: ....

NOTES: ....

_____

RECIPE STRIKEOUTS

They can't all be masterpieces!
Record some of your cooking mishaps.

WHAT I COOKED: ....

DATE ATTEMPTED: ....

WHAT WENT WRONG? ....

....

....

....

WHAT I COOKED: ....

DATE ATTEMPTED: ....

WHAT WENT WRONG? ....

....

....

....

WHAT I ATE: ....

WHEN + WHERE: ....

NOTES: ....

_____

WHAT I ATE: ....

WHEN + WHERE: ....

NOTES: ....

_____

WHAT I ATE: ....

WHEN + WHERE: ....

NOTES: ....

_____

WHAT I ATE: ....

WHEN + WHERE: ....

NOTES: ....

_____

WHAT I ATE: ....

WHEN + WHERE: ....

NOTES: ....

_____

WHAT I ATE: ....

WHEN + WHERE: ....

NOTES: ....

_____

WHAT I ATE: ....

WHEN + WHERE: ....

NOTES: ....

_____

WHAT I ATE: ....

WHEN + WHERE: ....

NOTES: ....

_____

CHEESE
CAKE
CUPCAKE

WHAT I ATE: ....

WHEN + WHERE: ....

NOTES: ....

....

WHAT I ATE: ....

WHEN + WHERE: ....

NOTES: ....

....

WHAT I ATE: ....

WHEN + WHERE: ....

NOTES: ....

....

WHAT I ATE: ....

WHEN + WHERE: ....

NOTES: ....

....

WHAT I ATE: ....

WHEN + WHERE: ....

NOTES: ....

_____

WHAT I ATE: ....

WHEN + WHERE: ....

NOTES: ....

_____

WHAT I ATE: ....

WHEN + WHERE: ....

NOTES: ....

_____

WHAT I ATE: ....

WHEN + WHERE: ....

NOTES: ....

_____

OLD RELIABLE

*Everybody has one. Record your all-time
favorite cook-at-home recipe.*

RECIPE: ....

INGREDIENTS: ....

....

....

....

PROCEDURE: ....

....

....

....

....

....

....

WHAT I ATE: ....

WHEN + WHERE: ....

NOTES: ....

_____

WHAT I ATE: ....

WHEN + WHERE: ....

NOTES: ....

_____

WHAT I ATE: ....

WHEN + WHERE: ....

NOTES: ....

_____

WHAT I ATE: ....

WHEN + WHERE: ....

NOTES: ....

_____

FOUR

amazinG

Tacos

WHAT I ATE: ....

WHEN + WHERE: ....

NOTES: ....

_____

WHAT I ATE: ....

WHEN + WHERE: ....

NOTES: ....

_____

WHAT I ATE: ....

WHEN + WHERE: ....

NOTES: ....

_____

WHAT I ATE: ....

WHEN + WHERE: ....

NOTES: ....

_____

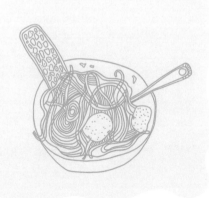

WHAT I ATE: ....

WHEN + WHERE: ....

NOTES: ....

_____

WHAT I ATE: ....

WHEN + WHERE: ....

NOTES: ....

_____

WHAT I ATE: ....

WHEN + WHERE: ....

NOTES: ....

_____

WHAT I ATE: ....

WHEN + WHERE: ....

NOTES: ....

_____

WHAT I ATE: ....

WHEN + WHERE: ....

NOTES: ....

_____

WHAT I ATE: ....

WHEN + WHERE: ....

NOTES: ....

_____

WHAT I ATE: ....

WHEN + WHERE: ....

NOTES: ....

_____

WHAT I ATE: ....

WHEN + WHERE: ....

NOTES: ....

_____

THE GREAT LATTE-OFF

*Try some new coffee shops. How do
they compare to your tried-and-true spots?*

SHOP: ....

NOTES: ....

....

SHOP: ....

NOTES: ....

....

SHOP: ....

NOTES: ....

....

SHOP: ....

NOTES: ....

....

WHAT I ATE: ....

WHEN + WHERE: ....

NOTES: ....

_____

WHAT I ATE: ....

WHEN + WHERE: ....

NOTES: ....

_____

WHAT I ATE: ....

WHEN + WHERE: ....

NOTES: ....

_____

WHAT I ATE: ....

WHEN + WHERE: ....

NOTES: ....

_____

BAG
OF
PEANUTS

WHAT I ATE: ....

WHEN + WHERE: ....

NOTES: ....

_____

WHAT I ATE: ....

WHEN + WHERE: ....

NOTES: ....

_____

WHAT I ATE: ....

WHEN + WHERE: ....

NOTES: ....

_____

WHAT I ATE: ....

WHEN + WHERE: ....

NOTES: ....

_____

WHAT I ATE: ....

WHEN + WHERE: ....

NOTES: ....

_____

WHAT I ATE: ....

WHEN + WHERE: ....

NOTES: ....

_____

WHAT I ATE: ....

WHEN + WHERE: ....

NOTES: ....

_____

WHAT I ATE: ....

WHEN + WHERE: ....

NOTES: ....

_____

SUSHI

WHAT I ATE: ....

WHEN + WHERE: ....

NOTES: ....

_____

WHAT I ATE: ....

WHEN + WHERE: ....

NOTES: ....

_____

WHAT I ATE: ....

WHEN + WHERE: ....

NOTES: ....

_____

WHAT I ATE: ....

WHEN + WHERE: ....

NOTES: ....

_____

VERSUS

Who wins? Who loses? Circle your favorites in these food match-ups.

DONUT (VS) BAGEL

PIZZA (VS) HAMBURGER

WAFFLES (VS) PANCAKES

TOAST (VS) CEREAL

BEER (VS) WINE

COOKIES (VS) CANDY

STEAK (VS) MEATLOAF

NOODLES (VS) RICE

LOBSTER (VS) CRAB

COFFEE (VS) TEA

PHO (VS) RAMEN

ICE CREAM (VS) GELATO

BREAD (VS) MUFFIN

TURKEY (VS) CHICKEN

MAYO (VS) KETCHUP

BUTTER (VS) OLIVE OIL

KALE (VS) COLLARDS

TOFU (VS) TEMPEH

BACON (VS) PROSCIUTTO

RYE BREAD (VS) WHEAT BREAD

ORANGES (VS) APPLES

.... (VS) ....

.... (VS) ....

.... (VS) ....

Sometimes I Love
to eat cinnamon
T O A S T.

WHAT I ATE: ....

WHEN + WHERE: ....

NOTES: ....

_____

WHAT I ATE: ....

WHEN + WHERE: ....

NOTES: ....

_____

WHAT I ATE: ....

WHEN + WHERE: ....

NOTES: ....

_____

WHAT I ATE: ....

WHEN + WHERE: ....

NOTES: ....

_____

WHAT I ATE: ....

WHEN + WHERE: ....

NOTES: ....

_____

WHAT I ATE: ....

WHEN + WHERE: ....

NOTES: ....

_____

WHAT I ATE: ....

WHEN + WHERE: ....

NOTES: ....

_____

WHAT I ATE: ....

WHEN + WHERE: ....

NOTES: ....

_____

WHAT I ATE: ....

WHEN + WHERE: ....

NOTES: ....

_____

WHAT I ATE: ....

WHEN + WHERE: ....

NOTES: ....

_____

WHAT I ATE: ....

WHEN + WHERE: ....

NOTES: ....

_____

WHAT I ATE: ....

WHEN + WHERE: ....

NOTES: ....

_____

string cheese

WHAT I ATE: ....

WHEN + WHERE: ....

NOTES: ....

_____

WHAT I ATE: ....

WHEN + WHERE: ....

NOTES: ....

_____

WHAT I ATE: ....

WHEN + WHERE: ....

NOTES: ....

_____

WHAT I ATE: ....

WHEN + WHERE: ....

NOTES: ....

_____

NEW STYLE

*Live a little! Break up your routine
and try new foods all day long.*

BREAKFAST: ....

NOTES: ....

....

LUNCH: ....

NOTES: ....

....

DINNER: ....

NOTES: ....

....

SNACK: ....

NOTES: ....

....

WHAT I ATE: ....

WHEN + WHERE: ....

NOTES: ....

_____

WHAT I ATE: ....

WHEN + WHERE: ....

NOTES: ....

_____

WHAT I ATE: ....

WHEN + WHERE: ....

NOTES: ....

_____

WHAT I ATE: ....

WHEN + WHERE: ....

NOTES: ....

_____

JASMINE
RICE

WHAT I ATE: ....

WHEN + WHERE: ....

NOTES: ....

_____

WHAT I ATE: ....

WHEN + WHERE: ....

NOTES: ....

_____

WHAT I ATE: ....

WHEN + WHERE: ....

NOTES: ....

_____

WHAT I ATE: ....

WHEN + WHERE: ....

NOTES: ....

_____

PEARS

WHAT I ATE: ....

WHEN + WHERE: ....

NOTES: ....

_____

WHAT I ATE: ....

WHEN + WHERE: ....

NOTES: ....

_____

WHAT I ATE: ....

WHEN + WHERE: ....

NOTES: ....

_____

WHAT I ATE: ....

WHEN + WHERE: ....

NOTES: ....

_____

WHAT I ATE: ....

WHEN + WHERE: ....

NOTES: ....

_____

WHAT I ATE: ....

WHEN + WHERE: ....

NOTES: ....

_____

WHAT I ATE: ....

WHEN + WHERE: ....

NOTES: ....

_____

WHAT I ATE: ....

WHEN + WHERE: ....

NOTES: ....

_____

ACCOUTREMENTS

What's life without a little sauce?
Draw your four favorite condiments.

1.

2.

3.

4.

peanut
butter
cups.

WHAT I ATE: ....

WHEN + WHERE: ....

NOTES: ....

_____

WHAT I ATE: ....

WHEN + WHERE: ....

NOTES: ....

_____

WHAT I ATE: ....

WHEN + WHERE: ....

NOTES: ....

_____

WHAT I ATE: ....

WHEN + WHERE: ....

NOTES: ....

_____

WHAT I ATE: ....

WHEN + WHERE: ....

NOTES: ....

_____

WHAT I ATE: ....

WHEN + WHERE: ....

NOTES: ....

_____

WHAT I ATE: ....

WHEN + WHERE: ....

NOTES: ....

_____

WHAT I ATE: ....

WHEN + WHERE: ....

NOTES: ....

_____

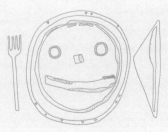

PANCAKE
FACE

WHAT I ATE: ....

WHEN + WHERE: ....

NOTES: ....

_____

WHAT I ATE: ....

WHEN + WHERE: ....

NOTES: ....

_____

WHAT I ATE: ....

WHEN + WHERE: ....

NOTES: ....

_____

WHAT I ATE: ....

WHEN + WHERE: ....

NOTES: ....

_____

WHAT I ATE: ....

WHEN + WHERE: ....

NOTES: ....

_____

WHAT I ATE: ....

WHEN + WHERE: ....

NOTES: ....

_____

WHAT I ATE: ....

WHEN + WHERE: ....

NOTES: ....

_____

WHAT I ATE: ....

WHEN + WHERE: ....

NOTES: ....

_____

LET'S GET CRITICAL

*Channel your inner food critic and
write a review of a recent meal.*

LOCATION: ....

MEAL: ....

REVIEW: ....

....

....

....

....

....

....

....

....

RATING (CIRCLE ONE): 1   2   3   4   5   6   7   8   9   10

WHAT I ATE: ....

WHEN + WHERE: ....

NOTES: ....

....

WHAT I ATE: ....

WHEN + WHERE: ....

NOTES: ....

....

WHAT I ATE: ....

WHEN + WHERE: ....

NOTES: ....

....

WHAT I ATE: ....

WHEN + WHERE: ....

NOTES: ....

....

WHAT I ATE: ....

WHEN + WHERE: ....

NOTES: ....

_____

WHAT I ATE: ....

WHEN + WHERE: ....

NOTES: ....

_____

WHAT I ATE: ....

WHEN + WHERE: ....

NOTES: ....

_____

WHAT I ATE: ....

WHEN + WHERE: ....

NOTES: ....

_____

WHAT I ATE: ....

WHEN + WHERE: ....

NOTES: ....

_____

WHAT I ATE: ....

WHEN + WHERE: ....

NOTES: ....

_____

WHAT I ATE: ....

WHEN + WHERE: ....

NOTES: ....

_____

WHAT I ATE: ....

WHEN + WHERE: ....

NOTES: ....

_____

WHAT I ATE: ....

WHEN + WHERE: ....

NOTES: ....

_____

WHAT I ATE: ....

WHEN + WHERE: ....

NOTES: ....

_____

WHAT I ATE: ....

WHEN + WHERE: ....

NOTES: ....

_____

WHAT I ATE: ....

WHEN + WHERE: ....

NOTES: ....

_____

HOLIDAY JAM SESSION

Record the best and the worst—the cream and the crummy—of your holiday meals and celebrations.

HOLIDAY: ....

NOTES: ....

....

HOLIDAY: ....

NOTES: ....

....

HOLIDAY: ....

NOTES: ....

....

HOLIDAY: ....

NOTES: ....

....

WHAT I ATE: ....

WHEN + WHERE: ....

NOTES: ....

_____

WHAT I ATE: ....

WHEN + WHERE: ....

NOTES: ....

_____

WHAT I ATE: ....

WHEN + WHERE: ....

NOTES: ....

_____

WHAT I ATE: ....

WHEN + WHERE: ....

NOTES: ....

_____

WHAT I ATE: ....

WHEN + WHERE: ....

NOTES: ....

_____

WHAT I ATE: ....

WHEN + WHERE: ....

NOTES: ....

_____

WHAT I ATE: ....

WHEN + WHERE: ....

NOTES: ....

_____

WHAT I ATE: ....

WHEN + WHERE: ....

NOTES: ....

_____

WHAT I ATE: ....

WHEN + WHERE: ....

NOTES: ....

_____

WHAT I ATE: ....

WHEN + WHERE: ....

NOTES: ....

_____

WHAT I ATE: ....

WHEN + WHERE: ....

NOTES: ....

_____

WHAT I ATE: ....

WHEN + WHERE: ....

NOTES: ....

_____

vietnamese
bánh mì
sandwich

WHAT I ATE: ....

WHEN + WHERE: ....

NOTES: ....

_____

WHAT I ATE: ....

WHEN + WHERE: ....

NOTES: ....

_____

WHAT I ATE: ....

WHEN + WHERE: ....

NOTES: ....

_____

WHAT I ATE: ....

WHEN + WHERE: ....

NOTES: ....

_____

INDULGENCES

Chocolate cake, french fries, sugary cereal?
Draw some of your favorite guilty pleasures.

1.

2.

3.

4.

WHAT I ATE: ....

WHEN + WHERE: ....

NOTES: ....

_____

WHAT I ATE: ....

WHEN + WHERE: ....

NOTES: ....

_____

WHAT I ATE: ....

WHEN + WHERE: ....

NOTES: ....

_____

WHAT I ATE: ....

WHEN + WHERE: ....

NOTES: ....

_____

GUACAMOLE

WHAT I ATE: ....

WHEN + WHERE: ....

NOTES: ....

_____

WHAT I ATE: ....

WHEN + WHERE: ....

NOTES: ....

_____

WHAT I ATE: ....

WHEN + WHERE: ....

NOTES: ....

_____

WHAT I ATE: ....

WHEN + WHERE: ....

NOTES: ....

_____

CARROT
CAKE

WHAT I ATE: ....

WHEN + WHERE: ....

NOTES: ....

_____

WHAT I ATE: ....

WHEN + WHERE: ....

NOTES: ....

_____

WHAT I ATE: ....

WHEN + WHERE: ....

NOTES: ....

_____

WHAT I ATE: ....

WHEN + WHERE: ....

NOTES: ....

_____

WHAT I ATE: ....

WHEN + WHERE: ....

NOTES: ....

_____

WHAT I ATE: ....

WHEN + WHERE: ....

NOTES: ....

_____

WHAT I ATE: ....

WHEN + WHERE: ....

NOTES: ....

_____

WHAT I ATE: ....

WHEN + WHERE: ....

NOTES: ....

_____

RESOURCES

PANTRY ESSENTIALS

Use this handy guide to make sure your cabinets are happily stocked.

OILS AND SAUCES:

- [ ] Balsamic vinegar
- [ ] Canola oil
- [ ] Extra virgin olive oil
- [ ] Hot sauce
- [ ] Ketchup
- [ ] Mayonnaise
- [ ] Red wine vinegar
- [ ] Sesame oil
- [ ] Soy sauce
- [ ] White wine vinegar

BAKING:

- [ ] All-purpose flour
- [ ] Baking powder
- [ ] Baking soda
- [ ] Brown sugar
- [ ] Chocolate chips
- [ ] Confectioners' sugar
- [ ] Granulated sugar
- [ ] Honey
- [ ] Maple syrup
- [ ] Vanilla extract

DRIED HERBS AND SPICES:

- [ ] Basil
- [ ] Black pepper
- [ ] Cinnamon
- [ ] Crushed red pepper
- [ ] Cumin
- [ ] Curry powder
- [ ] Garlic powder
- [ ] Kosher salt or sea salt
- [ ] Oregano
- [ ] Parsley
- [ ] Paprika
- [ ] Rosemary
- [ ] Sage
- [ ] Thyme

CANNED OR BOXED GOODS:

- [ ] Anchovies in oil
- [ ] Chicken broth
- [ ] Chickpeas
- [ ] Crushed tomatoes
- [ ] Tuna, salmon, or crab
- [ ] Vegetable broth

FRESH HERB GUIDE

*Add flavor, color, and aroma
with these basic herbs.*

BASIL: Sweet, minty taste. Use in pestos,
curries, sauces, and as a garnish. (1)

CHIVES: Mild onion taste. Use in dressings,
baked goods, and as a garnish. (2)

CILANTRO: Citrusy and clean taste. Use in sauces,
salsas, soups, and marinades. (3)

DILL: Sharp, tangy taste. Use in pickling,
dressings, and dips. (4)

MINT: Clean, strong taste. Use in cocktails,
jams, and dips. (5)

PARSLEY: Peppery and savory taste. Use as garnish
or in soups, stews, and sauces. (6)

ROSEMARY: Earthy pine taste. Use in baking,
marinades, and potato dishes. (7)

SAGE: Soft mint taste. Use in cream sauces
and meat roasts. (8)

IN SEASON

Fruits and vegetables in season by month.
This table may differ in some regions.

JAN:	Cabbage, Cauliflower, Leeks, Oranges
FEB:	Broccoli, Cauliflower, Lemons, Oranges
MAR:	Broccoli, Lettuce, Mangoes, Pineapples
APR:	Asparagus, Lettuce, Onions, Peas, Spinach
MAY:	Asparagus, Cabbage, Cherries, Leafy Greens, Lettuce, Onions, Peas, Radishes, Rhubarb, Spinach, Sprouts, Squash, Strawberries
JUN:	Apples, Asparagus, Beans, Berries, Cabbage, Carrots, Cherries, Eggplant, Garlic, Horseradish, Leeks, Lettuce, Melons, Nectarines, Okra, Onions, Peaches, Peas, Plums, Potatoes, Radishes, Rhubarb, Spinach, Squash, Strawberries, Tomatoes, Turnips
JUL:	Apples, Artichokes, Beans, Beets, Bell Peppers, Berries, Broccoli, Cabbage, Carrots, Cherries, Corn, Eggplant, Garlic, Grapes, Horseradish, Leeks, Melons, Nectarines, Okra, Onions, Peaches, Peas, Plums, Potatoes, Radishes, Rhubarb, Squash, Tomatoes, Turnips, Zucchini

AUG: Apples, Artichokes, Beans, Beets,
           Bell Peppers, Berries, Broccoli,
           Carrots, Cauliflower, Corn, Cucumbers,
           Eggplant, Garlic, Grapes, Herbs,
           Horseradish, Leeks, Lettuce, Melons,
           Nectarines, Okra, Onions, Peaches,
           Peas, Plums, Potatoes, Pumpkins,
           Radishes, Rhubarb, Squash, Sweet Potatoes,
           Tomatoes, Turnips, Zucchini

SEP: Apples, Beets, Bell Peppers, Broccoli,
           Cabbage, Carrots, Cauliflower, Corn,
           Cucumbers, Eggplant, Garlic, Grapes,
           Herbs, Horseradish, Lettuce, Melons,
           Nectarines, Okra, Onions, Peaches, Peas,
           Plums, Potatoes, Pumpkins, Radishes,
           Rhubarb, Spinach, Squash, Sweet Potatoes,
           Tomatoes, Turnips, Zucchini

OCT: Apples, Beets, Bell Peppers, Broccoi,
           Cabbage, Cauliflower, Corn, Cucumbers,
           Eggplant, Garlic, Grapes, Greens, Herbs,
           Horseradish, Lettuce, Okra, Onions,
           Peas, Plums, Potatoes, Pumpkins, Radishes,
           Rhubarb, Spinach, Sweet Potatoes, Squash,
           Tomatoes, Turnips

NOV: Apples, Bell Peppers, Cabbage,
           Garlic, Greens, Horseradish, Onions,
           Peas, Potatoes, Pumpkins, Spinach,
           Squash, Sweet Potatoes

DEC: Beets, Brussels Sprouts, Carrots, Oranges

COOKING CONVERSIONS

Know your ABC's of the TSPS (and the ozs).

1 TSP.	⅙ FL. OZ.	⅓ TBSP.
1 TBSP.	½ FL. OZ.	3 TSP.
⅛ CUP	1 FL. OZ.	2 TBSP.
¼ CUP	2 FL. OZ.	4 TBSP.
⅓ CUP	2¾ FL. OZ.	¼ CUP PLUS 4 TSP.
½ CUP	4 FL. OZ.	8 TBSP.
1 CUP	8 FL. OZ.	½ PINT
1 PINT	16 FL. OZ.	2 CUPS
1 QUART	32 FL. OZ.	2 PINTS
1 LITER	34 FL. OZ.	1 QUART PLUS ¼ CUP
1 GALLON	128 FL. OZ.	4 QUARTS

SUPERLATIVES

List your favorite food spots around town.

BAKERY: ....   KOREAN: ....

BAR: ....   NOODLES: ....

BRUNCH: ....   PIZZA: ....

BURGER: ....   SANDWICH: ....

BURRITO: ....   SEAFOOD: ....

COFFEE: ....   SUSHI: ....

FALAFEL: ....   THAI: ....

FRENCH: ....   VEGETARIAN: ....

FRIED CHICKEN: ....   VIETNAMESE: ....

ICE CREAM: ....

INDIAN: ....

ITALIAN: ....

ABOUT THE AUTHOR

Kate Bingaman-Burt is an
illustrator, educator, and maker of
things based in Portland, Oregon.
She is the author of Obsessive
Consumption: What Did You Buy Today? and
the What Did I Buy Today? journal.

Princeton Architectural Press
37 East Seventh Street
New York, New York 10003
www.papress.com

© 2014 Princeton Architectural Press.
All rights reserved. No part of this book
may be used or reproduced in any manner
without written permission from the publisher,
except in the context of reviews.

ISBN 978-1-61689-240-1

Manufactured in China

10 9 8 7 6 5 4 3 2 1

Editor: Jay Sacher
Designer: Elana Schlenker

SKILLET BRAISE

FRY STEAM tablespoon SNACK

GREENS POACH YUM!

Plate Knife BAKE

MANGIA DINNER

medium-rare BREAKFAST

TEASPOON FAT QUART

DINNER GRAVY

LUNCH SUGAR